The Wild Swans

De ville svanene

Bilingual picture book based on a fairy tale by

Hans Christian Andersen

Ulrich Renz · Marc Robitzky

The Wild Swans

De ville svanene

Bilingual picture book based on a fairy tale by

Hans Christian Andersen

Translation:

Ludwig Blohm, Pete Savill (English)

Ursula Johanna Aas (Norwegian)

Download audiobook at:

www.sefa-bilingual.com/mp3

Password for free access:

English: **WSEN1423**

Norwegian: **WSNO2324**

Once upon a time there were twelve royal children –
eleven brothers and one older sister, Elisa. They lived
happily in a beautiful castle.

Det var en gang tolv kongsbarn – elleve brødre og en
storesøster. Hun het Elisa. De levde lykkelig i et
vidunderlig slott.

One day the mother died, and some time later the king
married again. The new wife, however, was an evil witch.
She turned the eleven princes into swans and sent them far
away to a distant land beyond the large forest.

En dag døde moren, og en stund senere giftet kongen seg på nytt. Men den nye konen var en ond heks. Hun forhekset de elleve prinsene til svaner og sendte dem langt av gårde, til et fjernt land på den andre siden av den store skogen.

She dressed the girl in rags and smeared an ointment onto her face that turned her so ugly, that even her own father no longer recognized her and chased her out of the castle. Elisa ran into the dark forest.

Jenta kledde hun i filler og smurte ansiktet hennes inn med en stygg salve, slik at hennes egen far ikke lenger kjente henne igjen og jaget henne ut fra slottet. Elisa løp inn i den mørke skogen.

Now she was all alone, and longed for her missing brothers from the depths of her soul. As the evening came, she made herself a bed of moss under the trees.

Nå var hun helt alene og lengtet av hele sitt hjerte etter sine forsvunne brødre. Da det ble kveld, lagde hun seg en seng av mose under trærne.

The next morning she came to a calm lake and was shocked when she saw her reflection in it. But once she had washed, she was the most beautiful princess under the sun.

Neste morgen kom hun til en blikkstille innsjø og ble forskremt da hun så speilbildet sitt i vannet. Etter at hun hadde fått vasket seg, ble hun det vakreste kongsbarn på jorden.

After many days Elisa reached the great sea. Eleven swan feathers were bobbing on the waves.

Etter mange dager kom hun fram til havet. På bølgene gynget elleve svanefjær.

As the sun set, there was a swooshing noise in the air and eleven wild swans landed on the water. Elisa immediately recognized her enchanted brothers. They spoke swan language and because of this she could not understand them.

Ved solnedgang kjentes et brus i luften, og elleve ville svaner
landet på vannet. Elisa gjenkjente sine forheksede brødre
med en gang. Men fordi de bare snakket svanespråket,
kunne hun ikke forstå dem.

During the day the swans flew away, and at night the siblings snuggled up together in a cave.

One night Elisa had a strange dream: Her mother told her how she could release her brothers from the spell. She should knit shirts from stinging nettles and throw one over each of the swans. Until then, however, she was not allowed to speak a word, or else her brothers would die.
Elisa set to work immediately. Although her hands were burning as if they were on fire, she carried on knitting tirelessly.

Om dagen fløy svanene bort, men om natten krøp alle søsknene tett sammen i en grotte.

En natt drømte Elisa noe merkelig: Moren hennes fortalte henne hvordan hun kunne befri brødrene sine. Av brennesle skulle hun strikke en skjorte til hver svane og kaste dem over dem. Men fram til da måtte hun ikke si et eneste ord, ellers ville brødrene hennes dø.
Elisa startet å arbeide med en gang. Selv om hendene hennes sved som ild, strikket hun iherdig videre.

One day hunting horns sounded in the distance. A prince came riding along with his entourage and he soon stood in front of her. As they looked into each other's eyes, thcy fell in love.

En dag lød det jakthorn i det fjerne. En prins kom ridende med følget sitt, og om ikke lenge sto han foran henne. De ble forelsket i hverandre ved første blikk.

The prince lifted Elisa onto his horse and rode to his castle with her.

Prinsen løftet Elisa opp på hesten sin og red med henne til slottet sitt.

The mighty treasurer was anything but pleased with the arrival of the silent beauty. His own daughter was meant to become the prince's bride.

Den mektige skattmesteren var ikke særlig begeistret for den tause skjønnhetens ankomst. Han hadde tenkt seg sin egen datter som brud for prinsen.

Elisa had not forgotten her brothers. Every evening she continued working on the shirts. One night she went out to the cemetery to gather fresh nettles. While doing so she was secretly watched by the treasurer.

Elisa hadde ikke glemt brødrene sine. Hver kveld jobbet hun videre med skjortene. En natt gikk hun ut på kirkegården for å hente frisk brennesle. Skattmesteren hold øye med henne i skjul.

As soon as the prince was away on a hunting trip, the treasurer had Elisa thrown into the dungeon. He claimed that she was a witch who met with other witches at night.

Straks prinsen var på en jaktutflukt, kastet skattmesteren Elisa i en celle. Han påsto at hun var en heks, som møtte andre hekser om natten.

At dawn, Elisa was fetched by the guards. She was going to be burned to death at the marketplace.

I grålysningen neste morgen ble Elisa hentet av vaktene. Hun skulle bli brent på torget.

No sooner had she arrived there, when suddenly eleven white swans came flying towards her. Elisa quickly threw a shirt over each of them. Shortly thereafter all her brothers stood before her in human form. Only the smallest, whose shirt had not been quite finished, still had a wing in place of one arm.

Bålet brant allerede lystig da elleve svaner plutselig kom
flygende. Fort kastet Elisa en skjorte over hver av dem. Snart
sto alle brødrene foran henne, forvandlet tilbake som
mennesker igjen. Bare den minste hadde en vinge istedenfor
en arm siden skjorten hans ikke hadde blitt helt ferdig.

The siblings' joyous hugging and kissing hadn't yet finished as the prince returned. At last Elisa could explain everything to him. The prince had the evil treasurer thrown into the dungeon. And after that the wedding was celebrated for seven days.

And they all lived happily ever after.

Mens søsknene klemte og kysset hverandre, kom prinsen tilbake. Endelig kunne Elisa forklare ham alt sammen. Prinsens lot den onde skattmesteren settes i fengsel. Deretter feiret de bryllup syv dager til ende.

Og er de ikke døde, så lever de ennå.

Hans Christian Andersen

Hans Christian Andersen was born in the Danish city of Odense in 1805, and died in 1875 in Copenhagen. He gained world fame with his literary fairy-tales such as „The Little Mermaid", „The Emperor's New Clothes" and „The Ugly Duckling". The tale at hand, „The Wild Swans", was first published in 1838. It has been translated into more than one hundred languages and adapted for a wide range of media including theater, film and musical.

Hans Christian Andersen was born in the Danish city of Odense in 1805, and died in 1875 in Copenhagen. He gained world fame with his literary fairy-tales such as „The Little Mermaid", „The Emperor's New Clothes" and „The Ugly Duckling". The tale at hand, „The Wild Swans", was first published in 1838. It has been translated into more than one hundred languages and adapted for a wide range of media including theater, film and musical.

Marc Robitzky

Marc Robitzky, born in 1973, studied at the Technical School of Art in Hamburg and the Academy of Visual Arts in Frankfurt. He works as a freelance illustrator and communication designer in Aschaffenburg (Germany).

Marc Robitzky, born in 1973, studied at the Technical School of Art in Hamburg and the Academy of Visual Arts in Frankfurt. He works as a freelance illustrator and communication designer in Aschaffenburg (Germany).

Do you like drawing?

Here are the pictures from the story to color in:

www.sefa-bilingual.com/coloring

Dear Reader,

Thanks for choosing my book! If you (and most of all, your child) liked it, please spread the word via a Facebook-Like or an email to your friends:

www.sefa-bilingual.com/like

I would also be happy to get a comment or a review. Likes and comments are great TLC for authors, thanks so much!

If there is no audiobook version in your language yet, please be patient! We are working on making all the languages available as audiobooks. You can check the „Language Wizard" for the latest updates:

www.sefa-bilingual.com/languages

Now let me briefly introduce myself: I was born in Stuttgart in 1960, together with my twin brother Herbert (who also became a writer). I studied French literature and a couple of languages in Paris, then medicine in Lübeck. However, my career as a doctor was brief because I soon discovered books: medical books at first, for which I was an editor and a publisher, and later non-fiction and children's books.

I live with my wife Kirsten in Lübeck in the very north of Germany; together we have three (now grown) children, a dog, two cats, and a little publishing house: Sefa Press.

If you want to know more about me, you are welcome to visit my website: **www.ulrichrenz.de**

          Best regards,

          Ulrich Renz

The wild swans also propose:

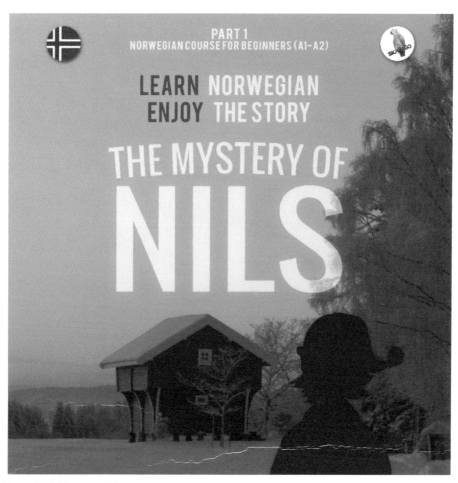

ISBN **9783945174005**

Learn Norwegian with a fascinating story!

Would you like to read a fun story while getting serious instruction in grammar and vocabulary?

Then you should have a look at "The Mystery of Nils" by Skapago Publishing. You can learn Norwegian with a coherent story that starts very simply, yet gets more and more advanced as the story progresses. Would you like to know how the story ends? If so.....you will just have to learn Norwegian!

For more information and a free preview see

www.skapago.eu

ISBN: 9783739909219

Sleep Tight, Little Wolf

For ages 2 and up

with audiobook for download

Tim can't fall asleep. His little wolf is missing! Perhaps he forgot him outside? Tim heads out all alone into the night – and unexpectedly encounters some friends …

Available in your languages?

▸ Check out with our „Language Wizard ":

www.sefa-bilingual.com/language-wizard-wolf

My
Most Beautiful Dream

Min aller fineste
drøm

Cornelia Haas · Ulrich Renz

English   bilingual   Norwegian

ISBN: 9783739962634

My Most Beautiful Dream

Recommended age: 3-4 and up

with audiobook for download

Lulu can't fall asleep. All her cuddly toys are dreaming already – the shark, the elephant, the little mouse, the dragon, the kangaroo, and the lion cub. Even the bear has trouble keeping his eyes open ...

Hey bear, will you take me along into your dream?

Thus begins a journey for Lulu that leads her through the dreams of her cuddly toys – and finally to her own most beautiful dream.

Available in your languages?

‣ Check out with our „Language Wizard ":

www.sefa-bilingual.com/language-wizard-dream

More of me ...

Bo & Friends

- ▶ Children's detective series in three volumes. Reading age: 9+
- ▶ German Edition: „Motte & Co" ▶ www.motte-und-co.de
- ▶ Download the series' first volume, „Bo and the Blackmailers" for free!

www.bo-and-friends.com/free

© 2019 by Sefa Verlag Kirsten Bödeker, Lübeck, Germany

www.sefa-verlag.de

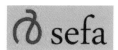

IT: Paul Bödeker, München, Germany

ISBN: 9783739971971

Version: 20190101

www.sefa-bilingual.com

Printed in Great Britain
by Amazon